SOCCER WORLD
SOUTH AFRICA
Explore the World Through Soccer

Ethan Zohn & David Rosenberg
Illustrated by Shawn Braley

ACKNOWLEDGMENTS

Ethan would like to dedicate this book to his brothers Lenard and Lee for showing him his first soccer ball; his first soccer coaches Aaron Zohn and Tony Tedesco; Rochelle Zohn for being the best soccer mom ever; Jenna Morasca for all her love and support; Delphine, Heidi, Ava, Adin, Oliver, and Isaiah Zohn; Kirk Freidrich; and the selfless staff, volunteers, interns, and students of Grassroot Soccer.

David would like to thank: Susan and Alex Kahan of Nomad Press for their support; Charlie Keegan for sharing his South African expertise and spirit; Stephen Jake Friedman, Craig Hayman, and Federico Fernandez; Harry Greenberg; language resources Betty Sibongile Dlamini and Debbie Makena; Josh Sundquist and Mark Hewlett for their continued optimism; and Lee Zohn for answering a random email many years ago. This book is dedicated to my kids Sam and Divya, to Ethan—who connects the world, and finally to my wife Suzanne Kent for her love and for seeing the writer in me before I did.

Nomad Press
A division of Nomad Communications
10 9 8 7 6 5 4 3 2 1

This book was manufactured by Transcontinental Interglobe,
Beauceville Quebec, Canada
February 2010, Job# 49054
ISBN: 978-1-934670-53-8

Illustrations by Shawn Braley

Questions regarding the ordering of this book should be addressed to
Independent Publishers Group
814 N. Franklin St.
Chicago, IL 60610
www.ipgbook.com

Nomad Press
2456 Christian St.
White River Junction, VT 05001
www.nomadpress.net

MEET ETHAN

WHO'S READY FOR AN EXCITING ADVENTURE?

My name is Ethan Zohn and I have loved soccer since I was 6 years old. As a professional player I have played all over the world. My favorite matches were in Zimbabwe, Chile, Israel, and Hawaii, just to name a few.

Soccer is played in almost every nation, so this game is like a common language that brings people together. I can just show up at a field with a ball and instantly make 20 cool new friends.

How would you like to come with me on my *Soccer World* adventures? We will meet young people just like you. They will share their customs and culture with us, like what they eat for breakfast and how to say hello in their language.

"Soccer is called football in other countries"

We'll learn about some special places and even what kinds of animals live in their countries. Along the way, we'll discover some fun activities that you can do in your classroom or at home.

So what are you waiting for? Grab your soccer ball and cleats and let's head out on our first journey!

VISIT ME!

Because you are my travel buddy, you can go to my website. See photos of the places we visit and find more activities and projects at www.soccerworldadventure.com.

THE RAINBOW COUNTRY

We are now flying to our very first soccer adventure in South Africa! From my home in New York City, it will take over 17 hours to get there. That is why I am so glad you are coming with me. Now I have time to tell you all about the country and the exciting places we are going to see.

South Africa is at the very bottom of the continent of Africa. It is a very large country, about the size of three Californias.

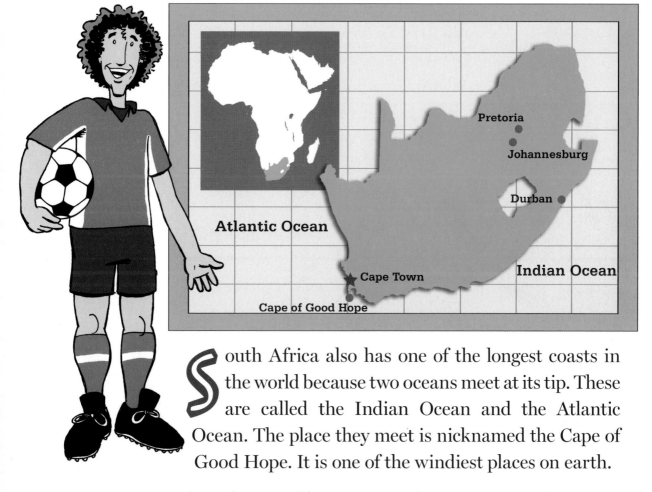

Atlantic Ocean

Pretoria

Johannesburg

Durban

Indian Ocean

Cape Town

Cape of Good Hope

outh Africa also has one of the longest coasts in the world because two oceans meet at its tip. These are called the Indian Ocean and the Atlantic Ocean. The place they meet is nicknamed the Cape of Good Hope. It is one of the windiest places on earth.

How many of you have nicknames? People sometimes call me "E," the first letter of my name, or "E-dog." When I played professional soccer in Africa they called me "Zo," which means "elephant" in the country that I was playing in.

South Africa's nickname is "The Rainbow Country." Is it because it rains a lot in South Africa, or because there are a lot of rainbows there? Actually, it's because a rainbow is made of many different colors. For South Africa, those colors represent all the different types of people who live in the country.

There are **ethnic groups** that have lived in Africa for thousands of years. Each has its own language and traditions. There are also South Africans whose **ancestors** came from other parts of the world.

SOUTH AFRICA'S FLAG COLOR

The flag of South Africa is the only national flag in the world to have six colors. It is also one of the newest flags, designed in 1994. The main Y shape in the flag is a symbol for unity between different groups of people.

WORDS 2 KNOW

continent: major land area.

ethnic group: large group of people with common ancestors and customs.

ancestors: people from your family or culture that lived before you, like your grandparents.

diversity: a variety of people from different backgrounds.

customs: traditions or ways of doing things, such as dress, food, or holidays.

culture: people with shared beliefs or customs.

safari: an adventurous journey or expedition.

Motto: "Unity In Diversity"

Today, people are learning to live together in South Africa. They are learning to enjoy new **customs**. It's important to focus on who people are on the inside instead of what they look like on the outside.

I bet you know people who come from different countries or **cultures**. Maybe a friend's parents came from China. Or another friend speaks Spanish or Arabic.

Because of all the cultures in South Africa, there are 11 official languages. That's 11 ways to say hello!

6

The cool thing about soccer is that I don't even need to know how to say hello. I can bring my soccer ball, and people of all ages, colors, and backgrounds are happy to play. It is through this beautiful game that I met my friend Tawela.

Tawela is eight years old and lives in Cape Town. Her ancestors are from the Xhosa tribe. Tawela is so excited that we are visiting her. She doesn't often have a chance to share her country with visitors like us.

"South Africa is a country filled with incredible places to visit."

We will see elephants and lions in the wilderness. Maybe we'll experience a night **safari**! We'll watch whales swimming and surfers catching waves in ocean bays. We'll even see places where cavemen drew picture stories on rocks.

Talking about South Africa with you sure has helped pass the time. Let's buckle up, because we're about to land in Cape Town. Tawela is waiting to meet us, and challenge us to a soccer game in the streets. Game on!

SOCCER IN SOUTH AFRICA

Soccer is the national sport of South Africa. So a visit to this country would not be complete without watching a professional soccer match and experiencing how passionate the fans are.

South Africa is the site of the 2010 FIFA World Cup. In this soccer championship, countries compete to be number one in the world. The FIFA World Cup happens every four years and 32 different countries make it to the final rounds.

The furthest the United States team ever went was third place. That was way back in the first year of the World Cup, 1930!

CRYSTAL CRAZY

South Africa is also famous for its rocks. Did you know that about half of the world's diamonds and gold come from this area? A diamond is a crystal that is made from coal under pressure for thousands of years. It is used for jewelry and is very valuable. It takes a lot of hard work to get gold and diamonds from inside the earth.

You can grow your own crystals. And you don't have to wait thousands of years to see the results! Have a parent or teacher help you.

The experiment will look like this when you are done preparing it. The pencil will sit across the top of the jar. Hanging from the middle of the pencil will be the pipe cleaner tied to the string. The pipe cleaner will be hanging into the colored water but not touching the bottom.

◊ pot for boiling water
◊ water
◊ 1-cup measuring cup
◊ glass jar
◊ tablespoon
◊ Borax soap powder
◊ food coloring
◊ pipe cleaners
◊ scissors
◊ string or twine
◊ pencil

1 Boil the water. With the measuring cup, pour the water into the jar. Keep track of how many cups it takes to fill up the jar.

2 Mix in 3 tablespoons of Borax for each cup of water in the jar. Stir to make sure most of the powder dissolves. Add a few drops of food coloring.

3 Bend your pipe cleaner into whatever shape you wish—a star, flower, or creation of your own. Be sure that your shape can fit into the jar opening.

4 Tie one end of the string to the pipe cleaner shape, then tie the other end of the string to the middle of the pencil.

5 Sit the pencil on the top of the open jar so that the pipe cleaner hangs down into the water. Make sure the pipe cleaner does NOT touch the bottom of the jar.

6 Wait at least 24 hours and then discover the crystals that you grew!

STREET SCENE

We are riding in a cab, called a *combi*, to Cape Town. This is one of the biggest cities in South Africa. South Africa has several large cities. Johannesburg, called Jo'Burg for short, is in the Northeast. Durban is on the East Coast. The capital of South Africa is Pretoria, also in the Northeast.

Hurray! I see Tawela and her friends through the window of the combi. I get out and we give each other a huge hug. Her friends have names like Zenzo, Mpumi, Siya, and my favorite, Kwinji. We are going to play a match of street soccer.

Before we choose sides, I notice that there are no goalposts. Tawela and her friends are also barefoot, which is the way lots of kids here play the game. Even though we are using my soccer ball, a few players have brought homemade soccer balls, created from rags, plastic bags, and string.

"Many South African children make toys out of recycled materials and random items they discover on the street."

Can you think of any toys you can make from items found around the house?

There are eight of us, so we divide into two teams of four: three players and a goalie on each side. Tawela and I are named captains and my luggage marks the goals.

Tawela is quite the **competitor**! She has great control over the ball because she dribbles it with both feet. With one quick move to the left, she scores a goal in the first minute!

WORDS 2 KNOW

recycle: to use something again.

competitor: someone trying to win or do better than others.

After a fun 15 minutes, I manage to shoot the ball past the hands of the goalie and tie the game 1-1. Although official soccer games last 90 minutes, I think a friendly tie is a great way to end the game. I am very tired from my long trip—and hungry!

After the game, Tawela invites us for lunch. We walk a few blocks to her house and meet her mom.

She is very kind, and reminds me of my own mom. She has made all of us a traditional lunch of pap and vegetables. I've worked up a big appetite, and clean my plate!

Afterwards, Tawela has a surprise. We are going to a traditional South African BBQ called a braai. The word *braai* rhymes with cry. Only men cook the different meats. These range from chicken and goat to many types of sausages.

CORNMEAL PAP

Pap is a staple food of South Africa and other African countries. That means it is served with many dishes. It is made of cornmeal—usually white but sometimes yellow. In the southern United States, a similar dish is called grits. In Mexico, cornmeal is used to make tortillas and tamales. Pap is called sima in Malawi and sadza in Zimbabwe.

Tawela's neighbors just got married, and the celebration spills into the streets. Even people walking by are invited to join the fun!

We all walk over to hear the music. Then I see Tawela whisper in the ear of one of the musicians. He has a big grin on his face as he calls me over to play in the band!

"I pick up a traditional African drum called a *djembe* and begin to pound out a beat in time with the music."

I am a soccer player, not a musician, but the crowd cheers me on. What a great first day in a beautiful land!

15

HELLO HELLO

Since South Africa has 11 official languages, now you can learn how to say hello in each of them!

ENGLISH Hello

AFRIKAANS Hallo or Goeiedag [HAH-low or HOY-uh-dahkk]

SESOTHO sa LEBOA Thobela [Tho-BEL-a]

SOUTHERN SOTHO (SESOTHO) Dumela [Doo-MEH-la]

SETSWANA (TSWANA) Dumela [Doo-MEH-la]

SWATI (siSWATI) Sawubona [Sow-BONE-a]

TSHVENDA (VENDA) Ndaa or Aa [Ndah or Ah]

XITSONGA (TSONGA) Avuxeni [Ah-boo-SHAH-nee]

NDEBELE Lotjhani [Lo-CHA-nee]

ZULU Sawubona [Sow-BONE-ah]

XHOSA Molo [MO-lo]

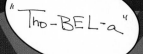

MAKE YOUR OWN PAP!

Remember what Tawela's mother served us for lunch? Now, you can make pap, too. Make sure you have an adult present when you do this.

Pap is like rice or mashed potatoes. It is meant to go with other foods, so you can serve it with vegetables or meat, or cover it with sauce or cheese. Some people eat it mixed with milk, sugar, and butter for breakfast! White cornmeal is usually used in South Africa to make pap, but if you can't find white cornmeal, yellow cornmeal will be fine.

SUPPLIES

◊ pot
◊ measuring cup
◊ 4 cups water
◊ 1 teaspoon salt
◊ 2 cups white cornmeal

1 Bring the water to a boil, and then turn the heat down to low. Add the salt.

2 Slowly stir in the cornmeal. Keep stirring until it is thick and all the lumps are out of it. Let the pap simmer for 20 minutes. Stir every 5 minutes. When you are done, the thickness should be like firm mashed potatoes.

3 Pour the pap into a bowl and then pair it with whatever food you've chosen.

FOOTBALL FRENZY

Soccer and Africa go together. In most African countries, soccer is the most popular national pastime. Everyone has their favorite team and follows it with passion and enthusiasm. South Africa is no different. In fact, the fans here are so excited about this sport, it's like their team is playing in the Super Bowl or World Series every week!

Football Frenzy

Today, after flying to Johannesburg from Cape Town, Tawela's family is taking us to Soccer City in Johannesburg. This stadium is designed to resemble traditional African pottery. It can hold over 90,000 people, making it the largest stadium in all of Africa.

"Can you imagine what a crowd as large as 90,000 people looks like?"

The next time you are at a sporting event, like your brother's high school basketball game or your family's next trip to a football game, find out how many seats are in the building, so you can compare.

When we first arrive, I am amazed by all the fans. Some have their faces painted with the colors of their team. Others wave giant colored flags. In Africa, some soccer teams have ties to ethnic groups, so it is almost like rooting for your family.

"Hosting the 2010 FIFA World Cup is a matter of great honor and pride for all South Africans."

It is great to see people from all different walks of life come together, have fun, and cheer for the same team. It doesn't matter if you are having a bad day or are worried about homework.

Even if you just had a fight with someone in your family or a friend, soccer can remind you of life's good times.

Football Frenzy

As the teams begin the game, the air is filled with chants and songs. Then I remember that the 2010 FIFA World Cup, the world championship of soccer, is taking place here this year.

This is the first time that an African country has ever hosted the FIFA World Cup, and everyone is very excited. While 197 teams enter, only 32 make it to the finals. I don't even know if I can name 32 countries. Can you?!

WORDS 2 KNOW

cooperation: working together.

communication: giving information from one person to another.

As we watch the two teams play, I see how much **cooperation** and **communication** occurs between team members. They have to trust and support each other.

"This makes soccer a good lesson for working with your own friends."

Our team wins, and its members high-five each other. They also congratulate their opponents on a great game. My voice is hoarse from all the cheering and chanting. I want to celebrate some more, but Tawela tells me that we need to get some rest in preparation for our trip tomorrow.

Where are we going tomorrow? Tawela smiles and tells me that it will be someplace wild.

FIFA

FIFA stands for the Federation Internationale de Football Association. It's like the government of world soccer. The name is in the French language.

MAKE YOUR OWN SOCCER BALL
JUST LIKE THE KIDS IN SOUTH AFRICA

1 This is like building a string ball or a tin foil ball. Start with the golf ball or rock at the center. Wrap it with a layer of rags. Tie it by winding the string around and around in all different directions. Tie the two ends of the string together with a knot. Wrap your ball with a layer of bags. Tie it in the same way.

2 Keep adding layers of rags and bags, tying each layer. Make sure your ball stays round and each layer is tied tightly.

3 Continue adding layers until it's the size you want it to be, like a small melon or an extra large grapefruit. Now think of a brand name for your ball and write it across the top with the marker.

SUPPLIES

◊ old golf ball or a small rock
◊ old rags
◊ lots of string
◊ plastic bags from the market
◊ marking pen

LOSE THE SHOES
SOCCER TOURNAMENT

It's good to raise your **heart rate** every day because it keeps your heart strong and your blood pumping through your body. You can do this by playing soccer—or walking briskly, riding a bike, or playing another sport.

Have some fun and get your heart rate up by playing a barefoot soccer match against your friends and family. Play the way they do in South Africa!

WORDS 2 KNOW

heart rate: number of heartbeats in a certain amount of time.

pulse: regular beat of blood pumping through your body. You can feel it either on your wrist or neck.

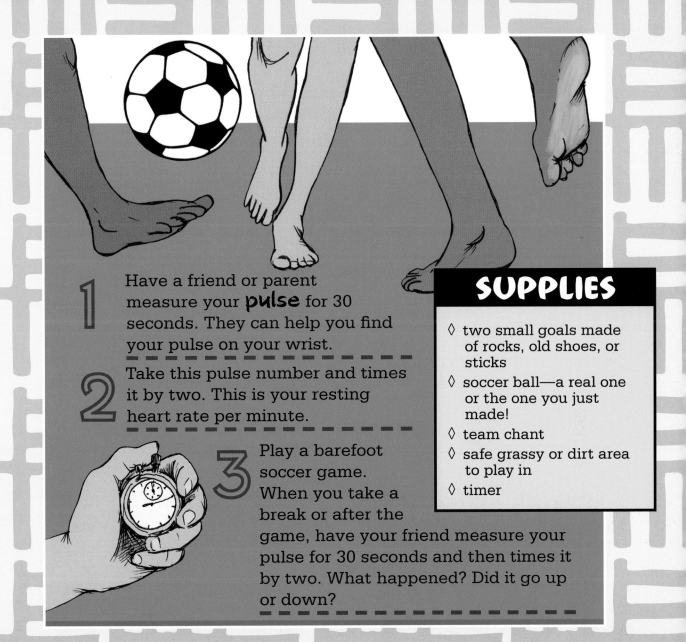

1 Have a friend or parent measure your **pulse** for 30 seconds. They can help you find your pulse on your wrist.

2 Take this pulse number and times it by two. This is your resting heart rate per minute.

3 Play a barefoot soccer game. When you take a break or after the game, have your friend measure your pulse for 30 seconds and then times it by two. What happened? Did it go up or down?

SUPPLIES

◊ two small goals made of rocks, old shoes, or sticks
◊ soccer ball—a real one or the one you just made!
◊ team chant
◊ safe grassy or dirt area to play in
◊ timer

INTO THE WILD

Can you guess why South Africa has very few zoos? Because most of the animals that you might expect to see in a zoo can be seen in their natural surroundings in South Africa. This is where they normally live.

Over the next week, Tawela is taking me to two very different places where we can observe and learn about animals.

WORDS 2 KNOW

preserve: an area where wildlife is protected.

savanna: a grassy flat area.

The first is a famous animal **preserve** called Kruger National Park, in the northeast part of the country. The park is enormous! It covers more than 7,000 square miles. That's almost as big as the state of Massachusetts. It is so big there are nine different entrances.

It is late afternoon as we climb into a jeep with our guide and drive toward the **savanna**. He tells us to look for a blue animal. Is he joking? I have seen bluebirds, but I can't imagine an animal with blue hair or fur!

KRUGER NATIONAL PARK

Kruger National Park has more than 140 kinds of animals. There are also over 500 different birds and 100 different reptiles. That's a lot of animals to look for, so I will definitely need your help!

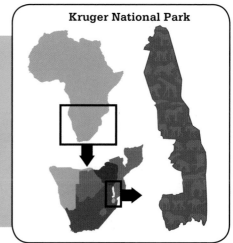

Kruger National Park

I am wrong. After a few minutes of driving, we observe a group of wildebeests whose coat is a shiny, silvery blue. They look like a cross between buffalo and elk. Their large horns curve in like the letter "C." Their special mouths allow the wildebeests to eat the short green grass that is hard for other animals to eat.

Many animals are best seen at night. We eat a light supper, then head out to watch the sunset and start the night safari. Luckily, we have night vision goggles with a green filter that allows us to see things in the dark.

"At dusk, we see some lions moving around. Elephants head to a watering hole."

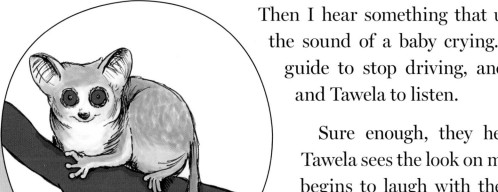

Then I hear something that upsets me: the sound of a baby crying. I ask the guide to stop driving, and tell him and Tawela to listen.

Sure enough, they hear it too. Tawela sees the look on my face and begins to laugh with the guide. Is this some sort of trick?

Tawela hands me the goggles and tells me to look carefully in the direction of the noise. I see a crying animal with huge eyes, claw feet, and a bushy tail. My friends tell me this is a galago. It is nicknamed a bush baby, because it makes the noise of a young wailing child. Even I have to laugh now!

AFRICA'S NIGHT SKY

As it gets dark, the night sky is so bright! You can almost reach up to the stars and touch them. I guess that's because there are no skyscrapers or lights from the city.

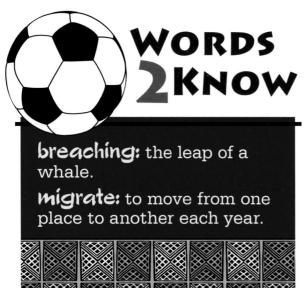

WORDS 2 KNOW

breaching: the leap of a whale.

migrate: to move from one place to another each year.

A few days later we visit the Western Cape area of South Africa. It is also known as Cape Whale Coast because it is one of the best spots in the world to watch whales.

There are over 29 different kinds of whales that pass this way, usually from June to September.

WHALES BREACHING

Whales move in groups called schools or pods. Tawela shouts "Look!" as one of them jumps fully out of the water. This wonderful feat is called **breaching**. A second whale uses its tail to stand on top of the water. Scientists call this skyhopping, but I call it awesome.

"The whales migrate thousands of miles from Antarctica and back again each year."

I could stay and watch the whales forever, but Tawela reminds me that there are other natural wonders for us to see. We are going to a place called Table Mountain and a surfing spot called Jeffreys Bay. We even get to see some mysterious art in the Drakensburg Caves. I'm so excited I might not be able to sleep tonight!

JOIN THE ANIMAL GANG

You probably know that a group of fish is called a school of fish. Do you know what a group of lions is called? Different groups of animals have different names.

Here are some of them:

lions............pride		giraffes.......tower
apes...........shrewdness		goats...........tribe
cheetahs.....coalition		gorillas.......band
deer..........mob or herd		hyenas........clan
dolphins.....pod		leopards......prowl
elephants...parade or herd		whales........school,
elk............gang		gam, or pod

MASK TASK

Many South African ethnic groups create ceremonial masks with animal faces. Now you can make your very own animal mask, too. This activity will take a few days to complete. You may want to ask for help from an adult, because this could get messy!

1 Cover your work surface with a towel. Put a few layers of newspaper over the towel.

2 Take some newspaper and tear it into strips. Torn strips work better than cut strips, so you don't need scissors for this step.

3 In the bowl, mix one part flour to two parts water. Add some salt. The mixture should be a little runny, like thick glue.

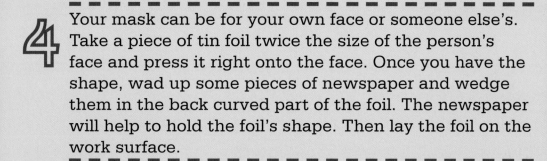

4 Your mask can be for your own face or someone else's. Take a piece of tin foil twice the size of the person's face and press it right onto the face. Once you have the shape, wad up some pieces of newspaper and wedge them in the back curved part of the foil. The newspaper will help to hold the foil's shape. Then lay the foil on the work surface.

5 Take a strip of newspaper and soak it in the paste. Use your fingers to squeeze out all the extra paste. Overlapping the strips, carefully cover the mask with one layer of pasty newspaper.

6 Let it dry for 24 hours. You can save your paste in the refrigerator if you have a microwave to heat it up the next day. Or you can make a fresh batch of paste.

7 Each day add a layer, until the mask is three or four layers thick. Once the mask is completely dry, you can paint and decorate it!

SUPPLIES

◊ towel
◊ lots of newspaper
◊ flour
◊ water
◊ bowl
◊ salt (a few tablespoons)
◊ tin foil
◊ paint and brush
◊ glue
◊ decorations such as, beads, feathers, glitter, and yarn

A COUNTRY OF NATURAL WONDERS

This morning we are climbing to the top of Table Mountain! It is called that because from a distance you can see it is flat on top, like a table. This famous **landform** overlooks Cape Town. Table Mountain rises 3,560 feet above **sea level** in the middle of the city. To give you an idea of how tall Table Mountain is, 1 kilometer is 3,280 feet. A mile is 5,280 feet.

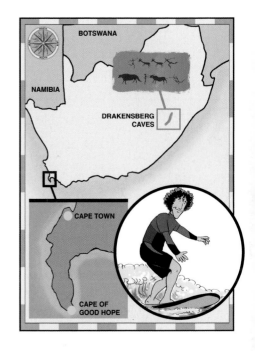

Tawela has packed a picnic lunch for the trek. She tells me there are hundreds of paths and ways to the top, but today we'll hike up and take the cable car down.

It will take us almost three hours to climb to the top. Fortunately, there are wonderful sights along the way. We'll see goat-like animals called rock hyraxes, and also baboons. We might even spot some people hang-gliding nearby, soaring in the wind.

Once at the top, we see the beautiful Cape of Good Hope. Looking out from Table Mountain, I feel like I am on top of the world.

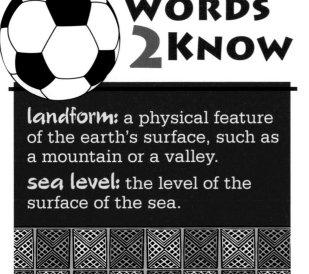

WORDS 2 KNOW

landform: a physical feature of the earth's surface, such as a mountain or a valley.

sea level: the level of the surface of the sea.

"A cape is a formation of land surrounded by water on three sides."

OCEAN TOPOGRAPHY

The topography is how the land is shaped along the coastline. It is also how the land is formed below the surface of the water, on the ocean floor. Features like sand shelves, reefs, and underwater formations are part of ocean topography. These affect surfing conditions. Waves are also affected by the direction and strength of the wind.

Later that week, Tawela and I go to Jeffreys Bay. This is considered one of the best surfing spots in the world. That's because of the way the waves form due to the ocean **topography**.

In Jeffreys Bay, the topography is perfect for surfing. Each section of the bay has its own funny nickname, like the Boneyard, which is a rocky area, and the Impossibles! Today, I am going to try surfing for the first time in the SuperTubes!

"Surfing turns out to be just like soccer, in that you don't need much to connect and have a good time."

Tawela asks her surfer friend Jake to show me how to surf. I am good at kickin' it on the field, but I don't know much about the water! Jake lends me a board, and off we go. I manage to ride a wave for a few seconds before I fall, curly hair now hanging in my face!

WORDS 2 KNOW

topography: different features of a surface, such as rocks, hills, and cliffs.

physics: the study of physical forces, including matter, energy, and motion.

matter: any material or substance that takes up space.

PHYSICS OF SURFING

A surfer's ability to glide on top of the water has to do with the science of physics. The surfer must be balanced right in the middle of the board and moving at the right speed down the wave, or else he or she will sink.

WORDS 2KNOW

sandstone: rock made of sand particles.

essence: most important feature.

At the end of the week, we visit the Drakensburg Caves. Some of the first people who lived in South Africa drew pictures on soft **sandstone** overhangs and cave walls. There are over 20,000 different pieces of art in this area.

We see walls covered with incredible carved and painted images of humans and animals. It is amazing that some of these drawings have lasted over 2,000 years. Can you imagine one of your paintings being found 2,000 years from now?

I wish that the paintings gave me the power to make our South African adventure last longer, but it is almost time for us to say goodbye.

DRAKENSBURG CAVE PAINTINGS

The people who created these cave paintings believed their artwork captured the life of the subjects, or their **essence**. In this way it gave them power over the animals they hunted.

SURF'S UP

Here is a physics experiment about floating and sinking. Combining an acid (vinegar) with a base (baking soda) makes carbon dioxide, a gas. In a liquid, gas bubbles can stick to the surface of a solid object. The bubbles lift the object up so that the gas can be released into the air.

1 Fill your container with three parts of water and one part of vinegar. Leave about an inch from the top.

2 Slowly add 1 teaspoon of baking soda. When the bubbling stops, add another teaspoon of baking soda.

3 Drop one of the food items into the water. It should sink to the bottom, then slowly rise to the top as the bubbles stick to its surface. The bubbles should pop at the surface, causing the food to sink again. Try it with different small food items.

SUPPLIES

◊ large glass container
◊ water
◊ vinegar
◊ baking soda
◊ teaspoon
◊ rice, raisins, or elbow pasta

Watching the hang gliders soar around Table Mountain got me thinking about cold and hot air.

Hang gliders are able to stay afloat because hot air rises. The sun heats the land, which then heats the air above it. As the air heats, it expands and rises, forming a **thermal**. Table Mountain has the perfect conditions for creating thermals.

Here is an experiment that uses hot air to get a whole egg inside a bottle! Since this involves matches and a cooked egg, you should have a teacher or parent with you when you do this.

WORDS 2KNOW

thermal: a column of warm air rising through cooler air.

1 Boil and peel an egg. Rub a little vegetable oil around the rim of the bottle.

2 Be ready with the egg. Have an adult light the strip of paper and drop it in the bottle.

3 Immediately set the egg on the hole, covering the hole completely with the egg. Watch as the egg gets sucked into the bottle!

SUPPLIES

◊ hard-boiled egg
◊ glass bottle with an opening just smaller than the egg—try a juice bottle
◊ vegetable oil
◊ matches
◊ strips of paper

Please be patient, this may take a few tries!

What's happening? The fire makes the air inside the bottle heat up and expand. But when the fire goes out from lack of oxygen, the air inside the bottle gets cooler and contracts, or gets smaller. This makes the air pressure lower inside the bottle than outside, and sucks the egg in!

SAYING GOODBYE

Tawela has been such a good friend and host. In every country I visit, I leave my host with something that is meaningful to me. Today, I give Tawela one of my game jerseys from playing pro soccer. It's a little big, but she will grow into it. Tawela gives me her homemade soccer ball. I tell Tawela to check the website for news, so she can keep up with all my travels.

Before I go, Tawela wants to teach me a few South African phrases as a souvenir of my trip. She introduces me to the slang term *lekker*, which means "everything is going well," and then tells me how to say thank you in her language of Xhosa, *enkosi*.

"Enkosi Tawela," I say to my friend.

WHERE NEXT?

I would love to hear where you think we should go for our next soccer adventure. Email me at Ethan@soccerworldadventure.com to share your ideas.

COUNTRY CONNECTION

In every country we visit, we want to make a difference for those who need our help. Gather your friends or classmates to find different charitable groups that benefit South Africa. Go to the Internet or a library. The cause that you choose can be anything from reducing poverty or increasing supplies of clean water, to preventing diseases like malaria.

Create a poster or a video to spread awareness about your cause. Do a report. Write letters to your friends about the organization. Or ask your parents if you can do some fundraising. You can have a bake sale, sell hand-drawn T-shirts or homemade bracelets, or run a lemonade stand. Get creative and have a fun event for everyone. What's important is not the amount of money you raise. It's that you are doing something to make happiness real for others and giving back to the world we all share.

Write a letter to your chosen group and tell them about what you've done. Include a couple of photos with a check. Let me know too. I would also love to see some pictures!

Glossary & Index

GLOSSARY

ancestors: people from your family or culture that lived before you, like your grandparents.

breaching: leap of a whale.

communication: giving information from one person to another.

competitor: someone trying to win or do better than others.

continent: major land area.

cooperation: working together.

culture: people with shared beliefs or customs.

customs: traditions or ways of doing things, such as dress, food, or holidays.

diversity: a variety of people from different backgrounds.

essence: most important feature.

ethnic group: large group of people with common ancestors and customs.

heart rate: number of heartbeats in a certain amount of time.

landform: a physical feature of the earth's surface, such as a mountain or a valley.

matter: any material or substance that takes up space.

migrate: to move from one place to another each year.

physics: the study of physical forces, including matter, energy, and motion.

preserve: an area where wildlife is protected.

pulse: regular beat of blood pumping through your body.

recycle: to use something again.

safari: an adventurous journey or expedition.

sandstone: rock made of sand particles.

savanna: a grassy flat area.

sea level: the level of the surface of the sea.

thermal: a column of warm air rising through cooler air.

topography: different features of a surface, such as as rocks, hills, and cliffs.